All th the world: A bittersweet poetry collection

Chanee Eliezrie

BookLeaf
Publishing

All the reasons in the world: A bittersweet poetry collection © 2023 Chanee Eliezrie

All rights reserved.

Presentation by *BookLeaf Publishing*

Web: www.bookleafpub.com

E-mail: info@bookleafpub.com

ISBN: 9789357212762

First edition 2023

To all the warriors out there, fighting your fight and getting back up after you fall — this one's for you.

ACKNOWLEDGEMENT

Big shoutout to my husband, Yosef, for his endless dedication, and to everyone who continues to support me in my writing journey.

Dictionary of compassion

If I had the words to heal all the broken hearts in
the world
I would, a hundred times over

I wish I had words to mend those broken seams
The tears shed, the hidden pain

If my words could heal, I wouldn't stop putting
pen to paper
I'd be scribbling pages of notes, poetry, prose

I'd give the world a message of hope
It would be wrapped tightly into a tiny scroll
And hidden in the unlikeliest of places:
A surgeons heavy paperweight
A toddlers favourite stuffed animal
A hospital patient's bedside table

But all I've got are my words
And while I can wrap them up tightly
Carry them in my fist like a forgotten treasure
— It's still all I have

So I'll take them — I'll take all the words I know
And turn them into a dictionary of compassion

I'll use them to my advantage
And hopefully — more importantly —
I'll use them to yours

Keeping her secrets close

I decided to write myself a letter
I'll start at the beginning
I'll talk to myself with love and compassion
The way I'd talk to my best friend

I'd only have nice things to say; comforting
things
I'd say things like "Look how far you've come,"
And — "You've got this, you can do this."

I'd feel my friend's pain, almost as if it were my
own
Help her fight her fights, battle her battles

I'd be there for her
The way a friend should be
I'd want the best for her
I'd want her spirit to soar

If I could take away her fear
I'd fill it with happy birds singing
And if I could take away her struggle
I'd do it with the utmost sensitivity

Keeping her secrets close
Trusting her with my presence
Letting her know it was ok

Whatever it was, it was ok
Whatever it was, it was ok

I hope you wake to sunshine

I hope you wake to sunshine
Catch that first glimpse of light through stained
glass windows
A kaleidoscope of colour

I hope it continues to surround you
Trailing behind you like an invisibility cloak
Keeping you warm; satisfied

I hope the light guides your decisions
Filters into the day's mundaneness
And washes over everything with sparkles

And when the night falls, I hope you go to sleep
content
Under a blanket of warmth and stars
I hope some of the stars slip under your cover
And tuck you in nice and tight and cozy

I hope you dream of beautiful places
With a whisper of hope on your lips
And nothing but peace in your heart

Light of day

Even if you feel hopeless and alone
And like the world is caving in on you
You will see the light of day again
Yes, you will

World of waves

In a world made of waves
I hope yours will always glitter

Hold on to faith

When nothing and everything makes sense all at
once
And all you need is a shoulder to lean on, hold
on

When you feel unexplained pain, and it feels like
too much to bear, hold on

And when you feel lost in this world of ours, lost
inside yourself
When your life feels like it lacks purpose, please
hold on then, too

In the good time, hold on
And in the hard times, hold on twice as hard

When you're tired and can hardly keep your
head up, hold on
And if you simply just don't know what to do
with yourself
These times please hold on the hardest

Hold on to hope
Hold on to faith

Hold on to yourself
Hold on to me

And please — please — don't let go

Yeah, life is alright

When the night is inky and soothing, and your
legs work effortlessly to move you forward
And your playlist feels cathartic in the very best
way possible
Things feel alright again

And when you pass the pizza shop that looks
like it belongs in Brooklyn
And see the workers through the window with
their perfectly round sections of dough
Yeah, life feels alright

When your night walk feels like you're in a
movie
And you've become the camera panning the
streets
Everything becomes a tiny bit special

It's like you're seeing the world through a new
lens
Things are falling into place around you
And the streets are alive with stories

When you notice your surroundings and feel at
one with them
The trees, the houses, the people, and even that
vast, inky sky
And they all feel synchronised to your mood,
clockwork style
Yeah, life is alright

Rollercoaster of memories

You know those times you're driving alone down
dark quiet streets
Maybe you're on the way back from a party or a
social event

You're feeling lonely and tired, wistful and
nostalgic
That feeling of knowing you want more
But being unable to access the emotions enough
to pinpoint them

And then a song comes on that sounds so
familiar it hurts
But you only realise why once the lyrics start
And then all at once you're back to where the
song takes you
Flying down a roller coaster of memories

And then you're crying
Because the song brings back so much
And the crying feels good
In the hardest way possible

You're in touch with something
That once meant a lot to you
And all your memories tumble into one

You crank up the volume, drive the final blocks
home
Think about life, hardship, happiness and
everything in between

And then you get home and turn the car off
The car goes silent
And you half wonder if you imagined the whole
thing

You go inside; get ready for bed
Take a shower and breathe

And somehow the experience feels cathartic
Like you needed it to happen

It's like the music and your emotions felt safe
To come out in the comfort of your car, driving
alone

As if you're the only one you could show those
feelings to
And like your car is the only thing that could
handle them

Rhythm

When it's dark
And the only thing
Propelling you forward
Is the rhythm of your heartbeat
—Take a breath

Like a thousand rushing raindrops

Come, it beckoned, step under me
Let me surround you and wash everything away
Allow me to be the one to catch your tears
Lean on me, let me touch you

The water, when I entered, was warm
But not too warm
Tilting my face to meet its embrace
It was everything it promised it would be

Comforting from the outside in
A curtain of water
Sparkling with a prism of colour

Reassuring as it pelted down
With a rhythm only water can fulfil:
It will all be ok
It will all be ok

As it washed away the memory of the day
Still imprinted on my skin
It conveyed the age old message:
I'm here, I'm not going away

I'm here to hold you
When you have nothing left to hold on to

Come, let me be there for you
Let me wash away your pain
Like a thousand rushing raindrops

Your hand in mine

Heaven and earth will collide a million times
over the second your hand reaches for mine
Even when you're falling
— Especially when you're falling
You will get up again

Do you feel any better now?

Let's go for a drive, I'll pick you up
We don't need to talk
But if you feel like it, I'm here to listen

I'll pick you up when you're ready
We'll go somewhere nice
Do you feel like ice cream?

I know you're hurting, honey
And that's ok
You are so much stronger than you think
And I know if I tell you that
You won't believe me
But that doesn't mean it's not true

You're not broken
And you don't need to be fixed
I hope you know that

I know you feel lost
Trust me, honey — I know
It's been an uphill battle
You can only carry so much
And I can see you're tired

So, let's go for a drive
I'll pick you up
We can listen to First Aid Kit
The music can stitch us together
Band-aid style

So, come, let's go for a drive
I'm here, I'm outside waiting for you
Let's go together
We don't need to talk
But if you feel like it
I'm here to listen

I'll turn on the music
We'll roll down the windows
Everything feels better with the wind in your
hair
Don't you think?

Let's go to the beach
Watch the waves out the window
Aren't they mesmerising?

The sun is setting
Do you see those blended colours?
It's a beautiful night
Perfect for a drive
Do you feel any better now?

Brighten the way

And in those times of darkness
When you feel lost, scared and alone
These are the times you'll emerge the brightest

Nothing shines brighter than those who have
seen the darkness
Lived through the blackest of nights

Souls on fire, flickering like candlelight
They rise

Umbrella

When the rain is coming down thick and fast and
heavy
And you're struggling to stay afloat
Allow me to hold the umbrella until your storm
is over

A prayer for you

May you be happy
Here
In this moment
With
Nothing more
And
Nothing less

A letter to my 5 year old self

You're five years old
Your emotions are bigger than you are
Things feel like they're too much
And maybe they are

You get lost in daydreams
Wrapped up in your own thoughts
You're a thinker, a dreamer, a believer

That knowledge that life is too much
And simultaneously not enough
Makes your heart feel too big
And your chest too small
There's something devastatingly beautiful about
it

You turn six, then seven, then eight
And then nine, ten and eleven
You can't turn the feelings off
And it still feels achey to live

Life is so beautifully bittersweet
And maybe that's how it will always be

Speed dial

What if everything you needed was at your
fingertips
Ready to be dialled into existence
What if you could dial one for connection
Two for happiness
Three for genuine love?

Would you remember your speed dial?

A patchwork puzzle of living

If I could heal the world with my own two hands
I'd take bricks of sorrow, layer them carefully
between bricks of happiness

The bricks of sorrow would be painted red, to
represent sacrifice
The bricks of happiness, a bright, blinding
yellow

I'd lay them down with care
Cushioned from anything that may scratch their
surface

Once complete, the wall would be layered with
happiness over sorrow
And sorrow over happiness
Like a patchwork puzzle of living

A testament to all that has been
And all there is yet to come

Life as we know it

You live it, you love it
You hate it, you fight it
But it doesn't go away
It's always that persistent thing tapping you on
your shoulder
Saying, 'I'm here. You can't ignore me.'

I'm already there

If the world was ending
You'd come over, right?

Yes, I'd come over so fast
I'm already there

All the reasons in the world

You have all the reasons
In the world
To be happy

So, my dear
What's stopping you?

Printed in the USA
CPSIA information can be obtained
at www.ICGtesting.com
LVHW020923061023
760263LV00038B/971